Hey

I'm Glad to Be Me

WRITTEN AND ILLUSTRATED BY P.K. HALLINAN

CHILDRENS PRESS, CHICAGO

Library of Congress Cataloging in Publication Data

Hallinan, P   K
  I'm glad to be me!

  SUMMARY: Examines reasons to be glad that you
are you.
  1. Self-acceptance—Juvenile literature.
2. Body image—Juvenile literature. [1. Self-
acceptance] I. Title.
BF697.H325   158'.1'024054   77-6327
ISBN 0-516-03509-6

7 8 9 10 11 12 R 85

I'm Glad
to Be Me

I've got two feet for tapping and dancing around,

and fingers for snapping some snap-happy sounds!

9

11

or stroll on a hill

in the warm summer sun with.

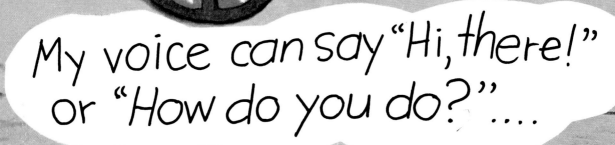

13

or talk in a whisper
with a close friend or two.

14

I can yell a big yell while I sit on a wall...

and a nose that just knows when some roses are near.

My shoulders feel cool
in a soft summer rain ...

ABOUT THE AUTHOR/ARTIST: Patrick Hallinan first began writing for children at the request of his wife, who asked him to write a book as a Christmas present for their two young sons.

Mr. Hallinan, through his charming text and pictures, shares with all children his delight in the world around him. He lives in southern California.